100 Years of
The Seaside
Twentieth Century in Pictures

100 Years of
The Seaside
Twentieth Century in Pictures

AMMONITE
PRESS

PRESS
ASSOCIATION
Images

First Published 2009 by
Ammonite Press
an imprint of AE Publications Ltd,
166 High Street, Lewes, East Sussex BN7 1XU

ISBN 978-1-906672-23-2

British Cataloguing in Publication Data. A catalogue
record of this book is available from the British Library.

Editor: Paul Richardson
Picture research: Press Association Images
Design: Gravemaker + Scott

Colour reproduction by GMC Reprographics
Printed and bound by Kyodo Nation Printing, Thailand

Page 2: Mr and Mrs
Everyman bask
in the Whit-sunshine
on the beach at
Bournemouth.
16th May, 1948

Page 5: Three girls
running through
the surf at Newquay.
15th July, 1955

Page 6: Jacqueline
and Rosie Reeder
on the beach at Looe.
2nd April, 2007

Introduction

The seaside holds a special place in the hearts of the British – which is both convenient and unsurprising for an island people that cannot, without leaving the country, be further than 70 miles from the coast. Notwithstanding this easy proximity, the seaside was the preserve of those who lived there – and the rich – until the 19th century. But then the railways came and the seaside, as we know it, was born. Quiet fishing villages became bustling resorts for thousands of trippers borne from Britain's cities and industrial centres to the beaches and coastline: the railway companies themselves were eager to fund this development as an investment in their passenger traffic.

The birth of the seaside was also the birth of the holiday for many: to be away from home and work, released from daily responsibilities, was a new experience for both the industrial working class and the new Victorian middle class. Thus the seaside was associated with pleasure, coming to represent a delicious, slightly naughty, fringe of British life. Around the beaches grew popular theatres, fairgrounds, pubs, arcades and piers – what piers were built from Britain's coast! – where holidaymakers could enjoy sights and sounds denied them in their daily lives. Men felt more dashing and ladies more glamorous: sensible clothes had no place there, instead our forebears paraded and caroused along the promenades in their most colourful and frivolous finery. By the end of Victoria's reign, a trip to the sea was the highlight of the year for millions.

The history of the seaside during the 20th century is a history of the most light-hearted and least pompous aspects of the British psyche, a story of kiss-me-quick hats and saucy postcards, donkey rides and sandcastles, bathing beauties and romance, children in rock pools and parents in deckchairs. And though its popularity waned as foreign travel came within the reach of ordinary people, the seaside's appeal remained and now grows stronger once more.

Fortunately the scenes on our beaches, piers and promenades have been diligently recorded over the years, allowing us to see this history for ourselves. In the pages of this book, through photographs selected from the vast archives of The Press Association, can be found a rare insight into the special relationship that we have with the seaside. These pictures tell us a great deal about ourselves – they show us how we looked when our guard was down.

Edwardian holidaymakers
enjoy the sun on the cliffs
near Folkestone.
1st July, 1909

Like nearby Ramsgate, Margate was a popular holiday destination for Londoners throughout Victorian and Edwardian times. It often features in writings of the period, mentioned by authors as diverse as William Thackeray and Karl Marx.

1st August, 1910

Four young women enjoy a
donkey ride on the beach
at Margate. The donkeys
seem less concerned by the
intervention of a dog than
their riders are.
1st August, 1910

A couple chat while seated on a sea bathing machine. These huts were towed into the sea to spare bathers the indignity of making their way down the beach in bathing costumes.

1st August, 1910

Brighton Royal Pavilion. The former Royal residence was
built in the early 19th century by designer John Nash, as a
seaside retreat for the then Prince Regent. This, together
with the establishment of rail links from London, transformed
the ancient settlement of Brighthelmston.
1st June, 1913

A small child rides in a
goat cart on the beach at
Seaview, Isle of Wight. Goat
power was much used at
seaside resorts of the time.
1st June, 1913

Two women paddle a canoe at the Isle of Wight. Behind them is the Seaview Chain Pier, one of only two suspension piers built: the other was at Brighton.
1st July, 1913

Lines of tents on the beach at Margate provide privacy for those whose sense of decorum demands it.
1st August, 1913

The Royal Navy's Home
Fleet anchored in Torbay for
the Review of the Fleet.
1st January, 1914

Facing page: A ladylike
swimmer enjoys the sea in a
suitably modest, voluminous
costume.
1st January, 1914

A woman wearing a figure-hugging bathing suit that would have been considered extremely risqué at the time. Photographers quickly realised the seaside's potential as a setting for glamorous, scantily-clad girls.
1st July, 1914

Holidaymakers relax in front of their tents on the shingle beach at Hove.
1st July, 1914

The very latest in bathing caps, costumes and wraps as designed for Harrods, modelled in this charming Margate snapshot that appeared in *Eve's Film Review*, Pathe Frere's weekly film review for women.
20th May, 1921

Miss Ena Beaumont, a film artiste and accomplished swimmer, strikes a diving pose before taking a header at Brighton.
14th July, 1921

Three of the competitors: (L-R) Miss Fidge (Italy) Violet Pout (England) and Berthy Egli (Spain), taking part in the first ever international beauty show held in Britain, at the Pier Hippodrome, Folkestone.

14th August, 1921

Eastbourne seafront. At this time one of Eastbourne's most popular tourist attractions was a small seaside cottage, scene of the gruesome and notorious Bungalow Murder in which an unscrupulous womaniser, Patrick Mahon, had done away with and dismembered his mistress, Emily Kaye.
3rd April, 1926

Lord Louis Mountbatten
with Lady Mountbatten
and her sister Mary Ashley
(L), bathing from the yacht
Shrimp.
1st May, 1927

Weir Club girls in bathing costumes enjoy the atmosphere at the Dobb Weir carnival in Hertfordshire.

6th August, 1929

They stopped the traffic: a policeman assists
a group of fashionable young ladies clad in the latest
beach wear – 'beach pyjamas' – as they cross the road.
1st January, 1930

Children perform sunbathing exercises at Hastings on the
Sussex coast. By the 1930s, heliotherapy – sunbathing for
health – was regarded as a public health measure: children
especially were exposed to the sun 'for their own good'.
1st May, 1931

St Michael's Mount. The buildings date back to the
12th century and have been a priory, fortress, a place of
pilgrimage and then, in the 17th century, a private home.
The site is now managed by the National Trust.
4th August, 1931

Facing page: Exploring
the cliffs at Holywell,
near Newquay.
4th August, 1931

Holidaymakers at Clacton enjoy the town's newly-built swimming pool.
19th September, 1932

Raparee Cove, Ilfracombe.
22nd July, 1933

Ilfracombe Harbour, around
which the fishing village grew
to become a thriving resort
town in the 19th century.
22nd July, 1933

The Duke of York, later King George VI, with Captain Patterson (L) after a bathe in the sea during a visit to his boys' camp at Southwold.
8th August, 1933

Facing page: One of the
Whitsun attractions at
Hastings in 1934 was a
boxing ring constructed on
a raft. Classes of young
girl boxers were formed
and their displays attracted
much attention from
holidaymakers.
20th May, 1934

The anchor from *HMS
Victory* displayed on the
seafront at Southsea.
22nd August, 1935

Young holidaymakers enjoy
a ride on the miniature
railway at Southsea.
22nd August, 1935

Fishing fleet and breakwater at Hastings. To this day Hastings has the largest beach-launched fishing fleet in Britain, as the town lacks a natural harbour. Although many attempts have been made to construct a man-made harbour, none succeeded.

24th August, 1936

Poole Harbour. The second largest natural harbour in the world, it was used as an invasion port by the Romans and has a history of continental trading stretching back to the Iron Age.
4th January, 1937

Facing page: The scene at Bournemouth where, drawn by brilliant sunshine, crowds seek entertainment and relaxation on the pierhead.
1st October, 1937

Between the wars an advertising campaign by the Great Western Railway Company was responsible for making Torquay a major resort. On the busiest day in August of 1938, 20,000 passengers arrived at Torquay station.

1st August, 1938

Holidaymakers climbing the rocks to get a view of the yachts during the annual Babbacombe Regatta, an event that has been held for more than 180 years.
1st July, 1939

Crowded scenes on Brighton beach in the month that wartime evacuees began arriving in the town and a general blackout was imposed. Less than a year later the beaches were closed to the public, mined and protected by barbed wire.

1st August, 1939

The West Pier boating lake at Brighton, after the town's beaches were cleared of mines and reopened to the public following the cessation of hostilities.
1st March, 1946

Ramsgate from the air. Here many thousands of soldiers
disembarked after escaping from Dunkirk in 1940: one of the
boats used in the evacuation is kept in the marina today.
1st June, 1946

Butlins holiday camp at Skegness was requisitioned during
the Second World War, during which it served as *HMS
Royal Arthur*. In the summer of 1946 it returned to its former,
happier role.
21st June, 1946

Gwenda Davies trained as a frogwoman to help with demonstrations at the Butlins holiday camp at Filey in Yorkshire, which had served as an RAF station during the war. Here she gets a light for her incongruous cigarette from two holidaymakers.
28th June, 1946

Facing page: Originally intended for adults, the Punch & Judy show became a children's entertainment in the late 19th century. Original members of the cast, including the devil and Punch's mistress Pretty Polly, were gradually dropped as being inappropriate for young audiences.
1st July, 1946

Most beaches on the south coast of England had been closed to the public for the war, strewn with barbed wire and mined due to the threat of invasion. To be able to relax at last in a deckchair on Bournemouth's sands must have been keenly pleasurable.

1st July, 1946

Facing page: Three holidaymakers sit on a capstan and look out to sea at the resort of Beer in Devon, reputed to have been settled by the crew of a wrecked Spanish ship during the time of the Great Plague when the local population was depleted.

14th July, 1946

Facing page: Ramsgate harbour showing fishing boats, yachts and launches. The Royal Navy used the port of Ramsgate as a base for Motor Torpedo Boats during the war.
1st September, 1946

An eight month old baby enjoys the first of many beach holidays.
2nd April, 1947

Holidaymakers cope with the
excitement of a sunny spring
day on Hastings Pier.
5th April, 1947

Facing page: A crowded beach in Bournemouth as
temperatures soared during a heatwave that lasted for six
days, with temperatures reaching over 30 degrees. It finally
melted the last of the remaining ice from an exceptionally
cold winter.
31st May, 1947

A row of chalets at
Skegness. Opened in 1936,
this was the first of Billy
Butlin's holiday camps.
2nd June, 1947

Facing page: A Butlins
Redcoat directs a guest
to the bathing pool at the
Skegness camp. Many
famous entertainers began
their showbusiness careers
as Redcoats, including
Des O'Connor and Sir Cliff
Richard.
2nd June, 1947

Scenes on the boating lake
at Butlins in Skegness. Later
that month Laurel & Hardy
played for a week at the
camp's Gaiety Theatre.
2nd June, 1947

Holidaymakers enjoy the
new outdoor swimming
pool at Butlins holiday
camp, Skegness. Post-
war refurbishment saw the
original complex updated
and improved.
10th June, 1947

Facing page: Two young women in bathing costumes run along the beach at Skegness. The east coast resort was the setting for many holiday memories thanks to entrepreneur Billy Butlin.
1st June, 1948

Children playing in the sand at Butlins holiday camp in Skegness.
1st June, 1948

Facing page: Two visitors from London's Bethnal Green paddle in the sea while on holiday in Bournemouth.
1st June, 1948

Holidaymakers watch a diving competition at the swimming pool of the Butlins holiday camp at Skegness.
1st June, 1948

Fun on the beach at Skegness. Nearly 60 years later Butlins would offer couples the chance to be married at the resort with an optional *Viva Las Vegas* package, complete with Elvis impersonator.
1st June, 1948

Inspired by the Eiffel Tower in Paris, Blackpool Tower was built at the end of the 19th century as the town became the most popular seaside resort in Britain. It cost £290,000 and took three years to construct.

26th July, 1948

A crowded beach at Southsea, as many people take advantage of a heatwave that saw one of the highest temperatures recorded in Britain during the 20th century.

30th July, 1948

Yachts during a Swallow
Class race at Torbay in the
1948 Olympic Games. K7 is
Great Britain's entry *Swift*,
Gold Medal winner in the
event.
3rd August, 1948

Girls with their surfboards make a dash for the rollers at Newquay, then and now the centre of surfing in Britain.
6th August, 1948

Facing page: Families enjoy the beach at Southend-on-Sea.
6th September, 1948

Facing page: Steamers at the quay in Great Yarmouth: fishing port, seaside resort and gateway to the Norfolk Broads.
23rd May, 1949

Blackpool Tower and seafront lit by 300,000 electric light bulbs during the first post-war illuminations. Special permission to consume the necessary power was granted by the government.
20th September, 1949

Choir boys scramble over the rocks with a Christmas goose for the keeper, William James, who waves a greeting at the approach to the Beachy Head lighthouse.
23rd December, 1949

Peacehaven, East Sussex, from the air. The brainchild of land speculator Charles Neville in 1914, Peacehaven is situated on downland to the east of Brighton.
1st January, 1950

Aerial view of Cleethorpes, at the mouth of the Humber estuary. A former fishing village, the town was developed by railway companies in the 19th century to serve as a resort town for holidaymakers from Sheffield.
1st January, 1950

Facing page: People enjoy the sun on the beach at Ventnor, Isle of Wight. Ventnor enjoys a subtropical microclimate and accordingly became a centre for the treatment of tuberculosis.
10th January, 1950

D Mottshaw and I A Bradley
playing chess on the beach
at Hastings.
8th April, 1950

Royal Navy destroyers pass unnoticed by the youth
of Plymouth as they enjoy the town's saltwater Tinside Pool.
The pool's distinctive semi-circular shape, projecting into
the sea, was a useful landmark for German bombers during
the war.
3rd June, 1950

100 Years of the Seaside • Twentieth Century in Pictures

Facing page: Blackpool
Tower sheds its brilliance
over the waterfront of
the Lancashire resort. In
this year the illuminations
were switched on by radio
superstar Wilfred Pickles.
16th September, 1950

Aerial view of the lighthouse
and promontory at
Flamborough Head, North
Yorkshire, one of the most
spectacular examples of
chalk cliffs in Britain.
10th October, 1950

Aerial view of Lulworth Cove
on the Jurassic coastline of
Dorset.
10th October, 1950

West Ham United footballers play leapfrog on the beach at Southend during training.
3rd January, 1951

Putting the finishing touches
to a town model in the
Seaside section of the
Festival of Britain.
30th April, 1951

Giant bucket in the *Seaside* section of the Festival of Britain. The Festival was a move to raise the spirits of the nation as it struggled to recover from the Second World War.

30th April, 1951

Facing page: Janet Sutton gives a long drink to Kathleen Brown straight from the siphon on the beach at Weston-Super-Mare. At the beginning of the 1950s, seaside beauty contests became an important part of the tourist draw.
4th August, 1951

June Beckett (L) and Shirley Boyer enjoy a ride on the donkeys on the beach at Weston-Super-Mare.
13th May, 1951

Not quite Blackpool, but a spirited show from the pier
illuminations at Southend Carnival and Festival of Light.
25th August, 1951

Douglas Harbour on the Isle
of Man. The Island enjoyed
a thriving tourist industry
until low cost foreign
holidays, with guaranteed
sun, became available.
19th May, 1952

Holidaymakers take a dip in
the sea with four elephants
from Billy Smart's Circus at
Weston-Super-Mare.
26th July, 1952

Facing page: Choppy seas
off the coast of Devon.
Hundreds of ships have
been wrecked in the area,
making it a mecca for scuba
divers.
1st August, 1952

The wreckage of the Beach Hotel, Sutton-on-Sea, after
a surge caused by the worst storm of the 20th century hit
the east coast. 24,000 houses were damaged, 300 people
drowned and 180,000 acres were flooded in a single night.

2nd February, 1953

Aerial views of Ryde on the
Isle of Wight. Ryde has six
miles of sandy beaches and
shallow waters – perfect for
family holidays in the 1950s.
15th June, 1953

Southsea's beach is crowded with people watching the Coronation Royal Naval Review of the Fleet, the first post-war Review, off Portsmouth on the Hampshire coast.
15th June, 1953

The *Big Dipper* at Blackpool Pleasure Beach. First opened in 1923, the rollercoaster was redesigned in 1936 but one section of the original ride remained in service until it was destroyed by a fire in 1953.
2nd August, 1953

With only a week to go until Christmas Day, the weather is so mild that these bathers can enjoy a pleasant lunchtime dip in the sea at Brighton.

17th December, 1953

Boxer Don Cockell (L), at Eastbourne before his World Heavyweight Championship fight with Rocky Marciano. Although Cockell lost in the ninth round, Marciano was full of praise for the Sussex farmer: *"He was a lot better than I thought. He's got a lotta guts, I hurt him somep'n awful"*.

28th May, 1954

Seaside fashion: Marcella de Cleves (L) wears a cotton sun dress and Jackie Howell wears a sun suit, while riding the horses on a seafront merry-go-round.
31st May, 1954

The beach at Shanklin on
the Isle of Wight.
5th July, 1954

Ventnor beach, on the Isle of Wight, as seen from the pier. Ventnor's pier was demolished in 1993 but not without a fight: the demolition rig broke from its moorings and its personnel had to be rescued by helicopter.
5th July, 1954

Facing page: Framing the pier at St Anne's-on-Sea as it races along the beach is a new sand yacht, controlled by engineers Orville Davis (L) and Millett Denning.
24th September, 1954

Coastguards during an exercise, in which rockets were fired over the sands to imagined stranded ships and rescues made by breeches buoy, near Winterton-on-Sea on the Norfolk coast.
21st February, 1955

Putting the beach back
where it belongs, after great
gales and high tides had
thrown up thousands of tons
of sand onto the promenade
at Great Yarmouth.
23rd February, 1955

The Snowflakes Sailing
Club, racing dinghies on
the River Thurne at Potters
Heigham near Great
Yarmouth.
15th March, 1955

Facing page: Seaford Head
cliffs, just around the corner
from the Seven Sisters and
Beachy Head on the East
Sussex coast.
4th May, 1955

Facing page: An aerial view of Blackpool Tower and beach.
1st June, 1955

Storm damage at Peacehaven, near Brighton on the East Sussex coast.
4th May, 1955

Pixie Carr out on Cooden Beach, Bexhill-on-Sea, with her shrimping net.
10th June, 1955

The beach and pier of Shanklin, Isle of Wight. The 1200-foot Shanklin Pier was opened in 1890 and the following year an innovative hydraulic lift to the clifftop above was added. The pier was destroyed in the 1987 hurricane.
23rd June, 1955

Taking a midnight dip
at Brighton: (L-R) Sylvia
Barnard, Jim Smith, Patricia
Mansell, Tommy Thompson
and Mary Jones.
13th July, 1955

A young woman poses for the camera at Great Yarmouth during a heatwave.
14th July, 1955

People enjoying the sun on
Brighton beach with the pier
in the background.
5th August, 1955

Ballet dancer Carol Masters enjoys a leap with Boozer, a champion boxer dog, on the beach at Bexhill.
29th March, 1956

Suzanne Crowley describes herself, with some justification, as a "*raving mad Dickie Valentine fan*". His voice goes everywhere with her on the records she carries with a portable gramophone. She made her hat from one of his records.
11th May, 1956

Yolande de Bonvouloir models a pink-and-white-striped beach suit from Horrockses of London.
21st February, 1957

Torquay takes no chances with its new multi-lingual sign, ensuring that even those from overseas will feel welcome at the South Devon coastal resort.
14th June, 1957

Fishermen and holidaymakers wave as the Queen and Duke of Edinburgh pass through Cobo Bay on the west coast of Guernsey during their tour of the Channel Islands.

26th July, 1957

Children's nurse Renata Waspi has her charge, Maia, slung safely in a bag as they examine their net for shrimps at Brighton.
16th August, 1957

An approximation of pop sensation Tommy Steele, in lights for the 1957 illuminations at Morecambe. The obligatory pretty girls are Audrey Cruddas (L) and Frieda Salmon.

19th August, 1957

Trying to see the sights
of Blackpool through
telescopes of seaside rock.
L-R: Phyllis Tollett, Valerie
Ansell, Dorothy Wallhead
and Marie Parker.
4th October, 1957

Stan Hawker leads a team of carthorses to collect the tons of gravel that are deposited every day on the beach at West Bay, Bridport.
12th October, 1957

Hundreds of tons of shingle were washed away by a gale-driven sea. Severe scouring of Sandown Castle, Deal, revealed a layer of chalk foundations: exposed, probably, for the first time since they were laid in 1539.
22nd January, 1958

Facing page: Sylvia Senior (L) and Diana Coote play with beach balls in a very cold February sea at Brighton. The two ladies are suffering in the cause of promoting the British Toy Fair, to be held during the following week.
17th February, 1958

Janine Glass stops the traffic with a large stuffed cat and an equally noticeable leopard skin coat on her way to the British Toy Fair in Brighton.
17th February, 1958

Young Shirley Downer plays with a covered wagon on the seafront at Brighton.
17th February, 1958

Desmond Goble tries out
a Super Multiple Shot Ball
Gun, assisted by Janine
Glass.
17th February, 1958

George, a penguin from Chessington Zoo, sizes up a giant toy penguin from the British Toy Fair, as their paths cross on Brighton seafront.

17th February, 1958

Determined sunbathers on Bournemouth beach in March
wear swimsuits while the rest of England is under snow. L-R:
Margot Oxford, Jean Bartlett, Lyn Harvey and Midge Brown.
9th March, 1958

Ann Bilham poses on Weston-Super-Mare's sand fire engine on the beach.
23rd May, 1958

Beach donkey Dorothy keeps an eye on her two week old baby Myrtle as she gives rides along the beach at Weston-Super-Mare.

23rd June, 1958

A miniature sand train on the beach at Morecambe. L-R:
Delyse Humphreys, Sheila McGaffigan, Dianne Coltman,
Patricia McHugh and Roberta Brown.
25th June, 1958

Beach cricket player Sheila Thompson after a game at Weston-Super-Mare.
26th June, 1958

Pupils of Scarborough
Technical Institute, taking
part in physical training
exercises on the town's
beach.
27th October, 1958

Sally Alford catches a rugby ball on the beach at Weston-Super-Mare.
28th March, 1959

Enjoying their first bathe of
the summer are Madeline
Perks (L) and Barbara Ray,
at Littlehampton.
10th May, 1959

A sweeping view of Fistral
Bay, Cornwall, famous for
its surf.
1st June, 1959

Meryle Watson enjoys the warm weather at Pevensey Bay with a spot of light shrimping.
18th June, 1959

A group of toddlers play with a pet chicken in the sea at Hove.
15th September, 1959

Young Gillian Skinner in a battle of wills with a recalcitrant donkey who refuses to gee-up, at Broadstairs.

25th September, 1959

Beach fashions from Littlewoods: Dawn Bailey (L) models a plain cotton stretch swimsuit with low back and high schoolgirl front, while Maddie models an elasticated cotton swimsuit with frills and ruched top.
18th February, 1960

L-R: Anita Jocelyn, June Russell, Valerie Cobb and Jean Anne Quill take a break from appearing in the Aqua-Revue at Bournemouth to enjoy some leisure time on the beach.
3rd June, 1960

Facing page: Holidaymakers cautiously view an unexploded 500 pound German bomb on the beach at Hastings. It had been brought in by the fishing boat *Little Paul*, which caught the bomb in its trawl.
9th August, 1960

Mr Douglas Hoare and his swimsuited daughter Patricia, painting a telephone box by the beach in Swanage. The pair work together for the GPO in Hampshire and Dorset maintaining postal boxes, telephone booths and police boxes.
20th June, 1960

Holiday motorists, picnicking
on the shore near Beaumaris
on the island of Anglesey,
watch the *St Tudno* sailing
along the Menai Strait.
31st August, 1960

Jill Simcox looks out to sea during a sunny spell on the seafront at Weston-Super-Mare.

7th September, 1960

Facing page: Captain Danion's sea lions reach for fish offered by Marie Sebright on the sands of Blackpool. The sea lions appeared on Ed Sullivan's television show *Talk of the Town* the following year.
6th June, 1961

Windmill girls Denise Warren (L) and Iris Chapple astride two pure white donkeys on Weston-Super-Mare beach.
31st March, 1961

Three showgirls taking a
break from rehearsals at the
Bournemouth Aqua-Revue:
(L-R) Diana Conroy, Valda
Clarke and June Russell.
23rd June, 1961

British film and television actress June Thorburn on the south coast, in the year that her film *Fury at Smugglers' Bay* was released. She appeared in many film and television roles during the 1950s and 1960s, including *The Cruel Sea*, *The Four Just Men* and *The Prisoner.*

1st July, 1961

Seagulls mug small
children on the beach near
Dartmouth.
18th July, 1961

Facing page: During a break
from the show *Take Pot Luck*
at the Morecambe Winter
Gardens, the Tiller Girls play
leapfrog for the camera.
5th August, 1961

A small boy plays with his bucket and spade at Boscombe beach, Bournemouth.
1st April, 1962

Children making sandcastles
at Boscombe beach.
1st April, 1962

Spring holidaymakers at
Boscombe beach.
1st April, 1962

People relax in deckchairs at Boscombe beach. Note the classic knotted handkerchief headgear in use, nearest the camera.
1st April, 1962

A woman takes a nap at
Boscombe beach.
1st April, 1962

Guy Barnett, 33 year old Labour candidate in the South Dorset Parliamentary by-election, canvassing a constituent and his dog on the windswept promenade at Weymouth.

7th November, 1962

The sea froze solid on the Kent coast in the Big Freeze of 1963: this was the scene at Minnis Bay, near Margate. The sea was frozen for three miles along the shore, a quarter of a mile out, during one of the coldest winters on record.
14th January, 1963

Facing page: The small town and cargo port of Fowey. Fowey has strong connections with the author Daphne Du Maurier, who spent most of her life in the area.
1st June, 1963

Two ladies relaxing in
the sun on the beach
at Newquay.
1st June, 1963

People relaxing and
sunbathing on the beach
at Newquay.
1st June, 1963

Children enjoy a ride on the donkeys at East Strand, Port Rush in Northern Ireland.
3rd August, 1963

Facing page: Feeding seagulls at Newquay.
1st June, 1963

A fashion show of French knitwear, swimwear and lingerie at the Mayfair Hotel. Steve wears a men's swimsuit with the athletic vest look, while Danik Patisson models the latest in ladies' swimwear.

7th October, 1963

Troops of the King's Own
Scottish Borderers searching
Palm Bay, Margate for
unexploded ammunition.
25th March, 1964

Police take away a young man as a large crowd of youths
gathers on the beach at Brighton. It was a scene repeated
many times as gangs of mods and rockers clashed at
seaside resorts during Bank Holidays, and recreated for the
1979 film *Quadrophenia*.
18th May, 1964

Sunlight and surf for the
dancing girls from the
summer show *Starlight
Rendezvous* at the Spa
Pavilion, Felixstowe.
6th July, 1964

Tony Spicer, official 'uncle'
to the thousands of children
who spent holidays at
Bournemouth, conducts
a balloon contest on the
sands.
6th August, 1964

Labour leader Harold Wilson enjoys a picnic on the beach at St Mary's, Isles of Scilly, with his wife Mary and sons Robin and Giles. This was the year in which Wilson first became Prime Minister, his General Election campaign being aided by the Profumo scandal.
20th August, 1964

Police officers watch a large crowd of youths during the Bank Holiday. The mods and rockers seaside riots of 1964 and 1965 presented the police with a situation they'd rarely met before, but which was to become a familiar aspect of law enforcement activity.

17th April, 1965

Facing page: Wheel Coates Bay near St Agnes, typical of the rugged Cornish coastline.

1st June, 1965

The threat of rain didn't deter
motorists from making for
Hayling Island on this June
day. With just one road on
and off the island, Hayling
has been host to some
spectacular traffic jams on
Bank Holiday weekends.
6th June, 1965

Children watch a traditional Punch & Judy show on the seafront at Walton-on-the-Naze.
1st July, 1965

Facing page: A view of Porthleven Harbour, the most southerly working port in Britain, showing its sea wall.
1st September, 1965

Ann Sidney, Miss World 1964, who in 1965 released the single *The Boy in the Woolly Sweater*, photographed at Butlins holiday camp in Bognor Regis.
24th August, 1965

Facing page: Holidaymakers look into the window of the village shop in Crantock, Cornwall.
1st June, 1966

The Dungeness Lighthouse in Kent. This structure was the fifth lighthouse to be built there, in 1961. The previous lighthouse still stands near to the new building.
1st September, 1965

Two of Great Britain's entries in the 1966 European Sand Yacht Championships, at Lytham St Anne's during practise for the event.
6th September, 1966

Facing page: Families enjoy the sun, the sea and the sand at Newquay.
1st June, 1966

Horses and their riders enjoy the sea air on the sands at Saltburn. Saltburn Pier is the most northerly surviving British pier and the last remaining in Yorkshire: in an exposed position facing north, it has been damaged and repaired many times since it was opened in 1869.

12th September, 1966

Neither dogs nor children would be likely to play in the paddling pool at Clevedon, with rough seas caused by strong winds and a high tide in the Bristol Channel.

16th September, 1966

Rough seas batter the
seafront at Clevedon.
16th September, 1966

A collection of swimwear and beachwear by Sabre of London.
20th September, 1966

All the nice girls... Crew from a French vessel, visiting Brighton as part of the Normandy Week celebrations, receive welcoming smiles as they stroll on the beach.
22nd September, 1966

Freddie and Jayne Fearn enjoy their Cornish holiday as they build sandcastles on the beach at St Ives. Most of the beaches that suffered from the oil spilled from the stricken oil tanker *Torrey Canyon* had been cleaned.
25th May, 1967

Facing page: A view of the putting green, beach and West Pier (now derelict) at Brighton.
15th August, 1967

Three girls play leapfrog for the camera at their local beach in Blackpool. The times were changing for Blackpool, however, Jimi Hendrix played the town's Opera House in this year.
15th June, 1967

Facing page: Thick oil stains the sand at Thorpe Bay on the Essex coast.
25th May, 1969

Sinbad the dolphin performing in a pool near Blackpool Tower. During the summer season he and his mate Pronto gave eight shows a day.
18th June, 1969

A hot weekend at Weymouth
brings everyone out on
to the beach to enjoy the
sunshine – the crowds are
just part of the fun.
13th July, 1969

Nine abreast on the *Astro Ride*, the latest import from America at the Pleasure Beach in Blackpool.
22nd July, 1969

ICI beach fashions: Sue Gellard wears a stretch Terylene Bri-Nylon cutaway swimsuit in turquoise trimmed with white, Chris Mason wears a beach shirt and trunks in striped stretch Terylene Bri-Nylon.

9th September, 1969

Irene Corrigan on one of the Victorian merry-go-round horses that her father, Albert Corrigan, is restoring. With his brother Jimmy, Albert founded a seaside dynasty that operates fairgrounds, amusements and tourist attractions, in Scarborough, Coney Island and Bridlington, to the present day.

13th December, 1969

Eight year old Geoff Wiffin of Hove carries off an armful of rock after he joined hundreds of other children at the House of Rock at Brighton.

16th May, 1970

Charlie Chaplin, as represented by Ronnie Collis who is appearing in the Ocean Show on Clacton Pier.
31st July, 1970

Holidaymakers queue to buy
ice creams on a hot summer
day at Cowes on the Isle of
Wight.
4th August, 1970

Watching the yachts sail by
at Cowes.
20th August, 1970

Facing page: Brenda Lloyd (L) and Rosalind Tyner endure an out of season paddle on the beach at Brighton.
16th January, 1971

Six year old Paul Shackleton at the helm of his own sand yacht at Brean Down, near Weston-Super-Mare.
14th April, 1971

Facing page: Southend Pier, the longest pleasure pier in the world, originally built in 1889. In 1974 the renewal of the pier's 1.34 mile walkway began: it was completed in 1979.

11th February, 1974

In a reassuringly familiar scene that could, were it not for the vehicles, have been recorded at any time during the 20th century, thousands crowd the sands at Blackpool beach during the hot weather.

15th July, 1971

(L-R): Jack Ward, Mick Birt, Roger Lumley, John Clinton and Peter Birt set out on an attempt to cross the English Channel on a bicycle-powered raft. Worsening weather forced them to give up after two hours. They should have waited: in this year work commenced on the Channel Tunnel.

28th July, 1974

Kenneth Wilkes launches
from a platform above the
sea in a competition to fly 50
metres at the International
Birdman Rally, Selsey.
10th August, 1975

The scene on Brighton
beach as temperatures
soared. This was Britain's
hottest summer since
records began, and with it
came a severe drought.
27th June, 1976

Not quite so crowded as nearby Southend-on-Sea, but nevertheless crowds were out on the beaches at Clacton-on-Sea for the Spring Bank Holiday.
29th May, 1978

In 1980, Brighton became
the first British resort with
an official naturist beach,
following much local
controversy. One Councillor
warned that it could become:
"*a flagrant exhibition of
mammary glands*".
4th April, 1980

Fully clothed skinheads seek refuge from the law in the sea at Southend. Police with dogs herded the London skinheads to the station to catch special trains home.
26th August, 1980

Conservationists demonstrate outside a Brighton hotel where the International Whaling Commission began a two day meeting to set catch limits for sperm whales.

24th March, 1982

As British Summertime nears, the donkeys at Weston-Super-Mare reluctantly start their work for the summer.
25th March, 1982

Facing page: New leader of the Labour Party Neil Kinnock and his wife Glenys are caught out by the waves on Brighton beach during a photo opportunity at the Party Conference. Seconds later Kinnock fell and was soaked, an event that dogged his career for years afterwards.
2nd October, 1983

Brighton remembers its Regency heritage, helped by Nigel Phillips, Brighton Belle Tracey Gunn (R) in period outfit and the new Miss Brighton, Frances Clarke.
7th June, 1983

Against a backdrop of industrial unrest and with coal supplies dwindling, these miners from Peterlee have returned to the ancient occupation of picking sea coal.

11th April, 1984

Escapologist Karl Bartoni
and his bride Wendy Stokes,
suspended from Blackpool
Tower for a blessing of their
forthcoming wedding.
27th May, 1985

Sharon the circus elephant makes friends with holidaymakers Graham and Janet Stead of Stapleford, on the beach at Great Yarmouth.
2nd September, 1985

Aborigine Burnum Burnum stakes his claim on England by planting his people's flag in the sand at Dover. As white Australians celebrated Australia Day, Aborigines dubbed it Invasion Day and declared a year of mourning for their stolen homeland.

26th January, 1988

C&A beachwear: Sarah (L) models a navy-and-white-striped vest with matching shorts, while Hayley shows off a white Matelot one-piece bathing costume.
22nd February, 1988

Youngsters line up for an
Easter Monday donkey ride
along a warm and sunny
beach at Weston-Super-
Mare.
27th March, 1989

Battling along the promenade at Blackpool was no fun as gale force winds lashed sand in the eyes and put the area on full alert with high tides expected.

5th January, 1991

A huge wave swamps property on the promenade at Blackpool as gale force winds and a high tide combined to cause havoc for those living near the sea.
5th January, 1991

Lifeguard Matt Holland
keeps watch over South Bay
at Scarborough.
6th August, 1995

The end of a summer heatwave came suddenly at Blackpool with squally showers and strong winds, keeping the tea stall quiet and making the beach a place on which to wrap up well.

24th August, 1995

Blackpool donkeys sagely consider the implications of Conservative defections to the Labour Party, at the start of the Tories' Annual Conference at the seaside resort.
8th October, 1995

On top of the world: Geoffrey Thompson, MD of Blackpool Pleasure Beach on the *Big One* ride. Mr Thompson became the first ever British President of the International Association of Amusement Parks.
18th November, 1995

Facing page: Filey's Cobble Landing and the town's fishing boats lie under a covering of snow after heavy falls affected the east coast.
28th December, 1995

A classic Spring Bank Holiday at the seaside: a troupe of entertainers trudge along the seafront at Scarborough, sheltering beneath an umbrella.
26th May, 1996

Children on the beach at
Weymouth as the weather
finally warmed up during the
schools' half-term holiday
week.
30th May, 1996

While the rest of the family head for cover, a father toughs it out with his sleeping son on a cold and windy promenade alongside the beach at Barry Island, South Wales.
23rd August, 1996

The scene on Blackpool
seafront after the pop group
Eternal switched on the
world famous Blackpool
Illuminations.
30th August, 1996

Facing page: Gary Miller
(L) and Gary Johnson are
among hundreds who braved
the freezing North Sea at
Sunderland's seaside resort,
Seaburn, for charity. The
annual dip, organised by the
Sunderland Lions Club, is
the biggest event of its kind
in the country.
26th December, 1996

A couple soak up the
summer sun on Margate
beach, in a quintessentially
British style.
31st May, 1997

Facing page: Almost July...
A deckchair attendant at
Scarborough waits patiently
while torrential rain, strong
winds and rough seas sweep
across the deserted beach,
forcing the closure of the
resort's Marine Drive.
26th June, 1997

Chris Hines, General Secretary of Surfers Against Sewage, makes a protest wearing a gas mask at Brighton on the third day of the Liberal Democrats' annual conference.
23rd September, 1998

Huntsmen from the
Holcombe Hunt exercise
their hounds on the beach
at Blackpool, as members
of the Countryside Alliance
took its manifesto to the
Labour Party Conference.
28th September, 1998

With Blackpool packed with visitors for the half-term and in the final week of the Illuminations, terrible weather closed the promenade. Earth movers, diggers and snow clearing equipment were brought in to move tons of sand, blown from the beach onto the tram lines.

29th October, 1998

An ancient oak circle, dubbed Seahenge, which emerged from shifting sands at Holme-next-the-Sea in Norfolk. The ring of oak trunks, with a large upturned tree at its centre, is believed to be 4,000 years old and of great archaeological importance.

14th January, 1999

Kareen and her older brother Yousef brave cold Bank Holiday weather to build sandcastles on a deserted beach at Blackpool.
31st May, 1999

Scarborough beach carries
warning signs to bathers,
alerting holidaymakers to the
dangers of stinging jellyfish
attracted by hot weather.
31st July, 1999

(L-R): Zani Gianluca, Miglietta Daniela and Francesco Guarino from Italy, who travelled to England to view the last total solar eclipse of the 20th century, wake up to cloud cover at Mounts Bay, Penzance.
11th August, 1999

Andrew Barraclough looks through a telescope on the seafront at Torquay.
11th August, 1999

Early morning sunbathers
on the seafront at Hove,
enjoying the benefits of
beach hut ownership.
28th August, 1999

A bather leaps from a wall and into the sea at Brighton beach, as the Sussex resort benefited from an unusual Indian summer with temperatures reaching 28 degrees.
12th September, 1999

Landscape artist Simon English works on a giant cartoon of a Tony Blair butterfly on Bournemouth beach. The artwork is part of a Friends of the Earth campaign to remind the Prime Minister of his promise of new laws to protect Britain's endangered wildlife.
24th September, 1999

Surfing dog Max riding on a surfboard on the beach at Broad Haven, Pembrokeshire. The Alsatian/collie cross was shortlisted for a Golden Bonio Award in a national competition.
1st March, 2000

Local residents prepare
for another wet and windy
Easter Bank Holiday on
Bournemouth seafront.
20th April, 2000

Maisie Lockwood, from
Shaftesbury, enjoying the
sun at Bournemouth during
the May Bank Holiday. Just
seven days earlier the Easter
weekend had been shrouded
in cloud and rain.
30th April, 2000

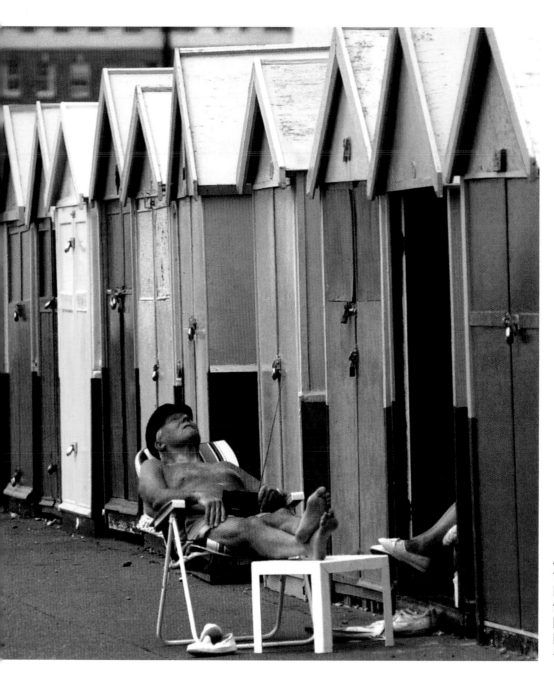

A bather optimistically hopes for sun in front of empty Brighton beach huts. Local flooding is predicted as heavy rain moves across England and Wales.
18th August, 2000

Doris Bell, aged 84, celebrates the opening of the *Lock and Barrel* with Drayman Arthur Wallaker. The seaside town of Frinton-on-Sea had resisted such modern amenities as fish and chip shops, pubs and seafood stalls, but finally gave in and allowed a pub in the High Street.

13th September, 2000

Work proceeds at the newly-extended pier at Southwold. It
was the first seaside pier to be built in Britain for nearly half a
century and cost businessman Chris Iredale £1 million.
5th April, 2001

Stephanie Calley enjoys the Bank Holiday as day-trippers flock to Weston-Super-Mare, where visitor numbers doubled over the Easter break due to the foot-and-mouth disease outbreak keeping holidaymakers away from the countryside.

16th April, 2001

Peter West, 77, from Southwold, takes an early morning dip in the North Sea every day during the summer and early autumn. Mr West used to swim around the former pier every day and reports that the new, extended structure takes him an extra 15 minutes.
3rd July, 2001

Battling against the weather
along Blackpool seafront as
the north of England was
battered by severe gales
and rain. More than 40 flood
warnings were in force.
28th January, 2002

Summer arrives on the beach at Scarborough at last, after a miserable start to the season.
15th July, 2002

Lyndsey Craig relaxes in
the sun on St Bees beach,
Cumbria.
4th August, 2002

Elvis tribute artist Michael King on the promenade in
Blackpool, during the Elvis Experience taking place at the
town's Winter Gardens, on the 25th anniversary of Presley's
death.
16th August, 2002

Environment Minister Michael Meacher leaves the water following a swim at Blackpool. Meacher had earlier pledged to take to the resort's waters once they met European standards – he did so during the Party Conference there in October.

2nd October, 2002

A trawler brings in its catch at Eyemouth harbour in the Scottish Borders. The small fishing town faced the threat of losing its only industry if a proposed EU blanket ban on cod fishing went ahead.

4th November, 2002

A policewoman clears members of the public from Brighton beach after a section of the town's historic West Pier collapsed into the sea overnight. Crowds scoured the seafront, taking pieces of driftwood from the pier as souvenirs.
29th December, 2002

Charred remains of the roller-coaster ride on Brighton Palace Pier following a fire. Dozens of people had to be evacuated, but no casualties were reported.
5th February, 2003

Peter and Jacqui Taylor working on their holiday hut at
Brighton seafront as the town enjoys a sunny Bank Holiday.
At the time the huts were changing hands for up to £8,500.
26th May, 2003

Eight year old James
Davies enjoys the beach at
Westbrook Bay, Margate,
after it was awarded a Blue
Flag for cleanliness.
5th June, 2003

The classic view of holidaymakers on the beach at Blackpool. In this week Britain's heatwave peaked with a temperature of 38.1 degrees, setting a new record.

6th August, 2003

People take to the sea to cool off at Margate during the heatwave that was responsible for some 35,000 deaths in Europe, 15,000 in France alone.
6th August, 2003

A mist obscures the derelict West Pier at Brighton. Health concerns were raised as the heatwave caused high levels of summer smog in many parts of the country. High ozone pollution was recorded by the UK National Air Quality Archive in many parts of London.
8th August, 2003

Facing page: Seven year old Shane Tandy from Weston-Super-Mare, who helps with the donkeys on the beach, feeds Jenny an ice cream during a break from giving rides to children on a hot afternoon.
10th August, 2003

Marc Tomes of Bournemouth at the moment of take off at the International Birdman Competition held at Bognor Regis.
31st August, 2003

Easter day-trippers take cover on Brighton beach, as rain showers speckled the south coast.
10th April, 2004

Deckchairs sit idle as the
sun beats down on the
Sussex coast.
31st May, 2004

Simple pleasures: children playing with windmills on the beach at Worthing during the Bank Holiday break.

31st May, 2004

A shopkeeper piles sandbags to protect her premises as gale force winds, high tides and torrential rain pound the beach at Scarborough. As Britain recovered from some of the worst summer storms on record, thousands of homes were still without electricity.

8th July, 2004

The Queen meets three lifeguards on Bournemouth Pier.
During her day at the seaside the Queen, accompanied
by the Duke of Edinburgh, also visited the Lighthouse Arts
Centre and opened a new Lifeboat College at the RNLI's
headquarters in Poole.
28th July, 2004

Traditional seaside fish &
chip shop fare: packed with
vitamins and goodness
to complement the healthy
sea air.
5th April, 2005

Sun, sea and pebbles.
Day-trippers on Brighton
beach enjoying the last long
weekend of the summer with
Bank Holiday temperatures
reaching the mid-20s.
29th August, 2005

Facing page: Lisa Connelly
soaks up the sun at Largs,
Ayrshire. The mercury
nudged 30 degrees at the
west coast spot, making it
one of the hottest places in
a Scotland that was enjoying
balmy Mediterranean
conditions.
19th July, 2006

A busy Bournemouth beach as people make the most of Easter Bank Holiday temperatures that soared well above average. Roads were jammed with people heading for the coast.
6th April, 2007

Facing page: Advertising boards for seaside cuisine at Brighton beach have been unchanged for decades – why spoil a winning formula?
24th February, 2007

Scarborough beach
holidaymakers over the
Easter Bank Holiday
weekend.
7th April, 2007

Clear blue skies over the
entrance to the pier at
Paignton.
8th April, 2007

Bank Holiday crowds at
the Grand Pier, Weston-
Super-Mare. Unseasonal
weather raised the spirits
and opened the wallets, with
British consumers spending
£3.5 billion over the Easter
weekend.
9th April, 2007

Facing page: Who needs
to travel abroad? A couple
enjoy the sunshine at
Sandbanks in Poole.
25th April, 2007

Beach huts at Sandbanks in
Poole.
25th April, 2007

Another Place, a group of over 100 iron sculptures by Antony Gormley on Crosby Beach, Merseyside.
9th June, 2007

A dream of freedom: a
camper van on a deserted
beach at Weston-Super-
Mare.
18th June, 2007

Facing page: An enduring
passion: generations
of children have ridden
generations of donkeys on
the beach at Weston-Super-
Mare.
18th June, 2007

Holidaymaker Ilka Fischer (L)
from Nuremberg, Germany
on the beach at Brighton on
one of the hottest days of the
summer.
5th August, 2007

Facing page: The
spectacular limestone
arch of Durdle Door, near
Lulworth on the Jurassic
coast of Dorset.
13th August, 2007

Holidaymakers take cover
under umbrellas on the
beach at Weston-Super-
Mare. Even in August, you
just never know what the
weather will do – it would be
boring otherwise.
15th August, 2007

Facing page: Fistral Beach
in Newquay, where the
finest waves in Britain are a
magnet for surfers.
16th August, 2007

Walking along the seafront
at Largs on the west coast of
Scotland.
10th March, 2008

Waves crash against the historic Cobb at Lyme Regis. The ancient sea wall features in Jane Austen's novel *Persuasion*, and John Fowles' *The French Lieutenant's Woman*: in a memorable scene from the film of the latter, actress Meryll Streep stands windswept upon it.

10th March, 2008

A wave breaks over the A956 in Cumbria as the north west of England was battered by strong winds, which caused disruption on the roads and damage to homes.
12th March, 2008

The beach and pier of
Bournemouth provide
timeless pleasure for
holidaymakers.
26th April, 2008

Puffins on the Farne
Islands off the coast of
Northumberland.
2nd May, 2008

Facing page: Enjoying the
British seaside sometimes
requires a certain
doggedness of spirit: very
character forming.
26th May, 2008

Skegness offshore wind
farm. When complete it will
be the largest offshore wind
farm in the world, its 54
turbines capable of providing
sufficient power for half the
homes in Lincolnshire.
12th July, 2008

Perplexed onlookers view a sand sculpture entitled *North America,* consisting of totem poles, bears, a hockey player, fir trees and buildings, by Jill and Thomas from Florida, on Weston-Super-Mare beach. The resort's sand has the perfect consistency for such sculptures.
12th July, 2008

A seagull harasses a holidaymaker. Seagulls became increasingly aggressive in areas where they were accustomed to being fed, leading to controversial culls.
14th July, 2008

A member of the public takes a picture of the Household Cavalry, the Life Guards Regiment, at Holkham Beach during their three-week summer training camp in Norfolk.

22nd July, 2008

The Grand Pier at Weston-
Super-Mare, the last of the
great pleasure piers to be
built, was devastated by fire
104 years after it was first
opened.
28th July, 2008

Facing page: Fire tears
through the structure that
was once Weston's pier. It is
hoped that rebuilding work
– likely to cost £30 million –
can be completed by 2010.
28th July, 2008

Children play on the beach
at Whitley Bay, oblivious
to storm clouds gathering
above.
2nd August, 2008

Fistral beach, Newquay, on the first day of the Rip Curl Boardmasters Competition. The event, the largest surfing festival in Europe, has been held at Fistral beach since 1981.

4th August, 2008

Competition surfer Adam
Melling from Australia sits on
the shore of Fistral.
6th August, 2008

Facing page: Tynemouth
Beach as rain continues
to fall during a miserable
August for Britain. Never
mind – there's always next
year.
18th August, 2008

The Publishers gratefully acknowledge Press Association Images, from whose extensive archive the photographs in this book have been selected. Personal copies of the photographs in this book, and many others, may be ordered online at www.prints.paphotos.com

For more information, please contact:

Ammonite Press

AE Publications Ltd. 166 High Street, Lewes, East Sussex, BN7 1XU, United Kingdom

Tel: 01273 488005 Fax: 01273 402866

www.ammonitepress.com